This Insubstantial Pageant

D1565808

Also by Estha Weiner

at the last minute
In the Weather of the World
The Mistress Manuscript
Transfiguration Begins At Home

Blues for Bill: A Tribute to William Matthews (co-editor/contributor)

THIS
INSUBSTANTIAL
PAGEANT

Poems

Estha Weiner

Broadstone

ISBN 978-1-956782-25-7

Text Design by Larry W. Moore
Cover Design by the author &
Larry W. Moore

Cover photograph by Elliott Kaufman,
used by permission

Broadstone Books
An Imprint of
Broadstone Media LLC
418 Ann Street
Frankfort, KY 40601-1929
BroadstoneBooks.com

CONTENTS

Our revels now are ended. These our actors,
As I foretold you, were all spirits, and
Are melted into air, into thin air:
And, like the baseless fabric of this vision,
The cloud-capp'd towers, the gorgeous palaces,
The solemn temples, the great globe itself,
Yea, all which it inherit, shall dissolve;
And, like this insubstantial pageant faded,
Leave not a rack behind. We are such stuff
As dreams are made on, and our little life
Is rounded with a sleep.

—William Shakespeare, *The Tempest*

All the world's a stage
And all the men and women merely players;
They have their exits and their entrances,
And one man in his time plays many parts...

—William Shakespeare, *As You Like It*

Life upon the wicked stage
Ain't ever what a girl supposes...

—Oscar Hammerstein and Jerome Kern, *Showboat*

Hell is Murky, 2020

A little water
clears us
of this deed

Will all great Neptune's
ocean wash this blood
clean from my hand?

Wash your hands,
put on your nightgown,
look not so pale

What, will these hands
ne'er be clean?

Here's the smell
of the blood still.
All the perfumes
of Arabia will not
sweeten this little hand

What need we fear?
Who knows it when none can call our power
to account?

'*A GREEN AND YELLOW MELANCHOLY*,'
not black and white:

Green: all that grows
with the help of the sun.

Envy, mold, and decay;
choleric bile and jaundice.

Green: from yellow and blue;
green: from yellow and black.

(The Blues, the mad,
the dark.)

A shamrock;
a star for Jews.

Greenbacks and acclaim from The Pulitzer,
named for a yellow journalist.

Wet behind the ears;
a yellow dog.

A frog;
a coward.

'Smiling at grief.
Was not this love indeed?'

*A*ND THERE'S STILL FREE *S*HAKESPEARE IN *T*HE *P*ARK

The stage rotates, complete
with moat and arc of bridge
for Montagues and Capulets and Princes.
This Juliet's red tresses glow
as the sun sets on order
of both directors. Sound carries in the night.
Suddenly, not from the stage:
"Sieg Heil! Heil Hitler!" stabs
our Shakespeare, sprung from a script
unspeakable, a prank
of punks. We hope,
and reel attention back
to Juliet, who might wake
in time, this time.

SLEEP, why
should anyone go to:

sleep, that knits up the raveled sleave
of care,
which Macbeth does murder,
through which his Lady walks,
with miles to go;

pray and then I'll

sleep, per chance
to dream

die, to sleep
no more

A LITTLE BECKETT, A LITTLE O'NEILL

The landscape is indeterminate
A woman opens her mouth; laughter
careens from her lungs
up into her throat
only to be choked
before its sound can escape
and change the air.
In the breeze of anticipated
summer is ice
that will become a man.

As I look down on you, I love you

from my back balcony
on your communal roof:

I view where you've placed
a rectangular table,

so humans can dine together
socially, at a distance, after 7.

First, you prepare the barbeque,
And set the table—

I like to watch you
turn each piece of chicken—

Then a salad bowl appears,
and then the wine,

other humans now
relishing the time.

Tall, lean, and elegantly greying—
Anthony Bourdain or Prospero—

Three nights a week,
you create the feast

which lasts beyond
the dark,

until it disappears

PERFORMANCE ART

You don't see this every day:
Two Nudes on Floor, on
Canvas, never more, at MOMA:

Two Nudes on Floor, face
Each other in between
Two exhibition spaces

Two models paid to stand
Nude on MOMA's floor
From opening to close

We nearly touch them
As we pass from one
Room to another

One girl, one woman
Stand nude and stare
Into each other's eyes

Nearby, the guard stands also
As he's paid to do:
He does not stare at the two.

He stands on MOMA's floor
From opening to close
With all his clothes on.

He'll be there
When the ladies aren't
Standing on MOMA's floor.

Untitled II

This is an environmental, not an interactive performance, so the guy sitting across from me at the table in the barroom that is the environment of the performance checks his phone, shoots throat spray into his mouth, looks up, looks down, checks his phone again, but never interacts. We're part of the audience. We're not in the show.

SWEET SONGS OF THE STREET

Extra, Extra, Read all About It!

Line up!

Wate me—
Wateme—
Watemellon!

Delicious Knishes!

They're so sweet and fine—
And they're right off the vine—
Strawberries!

Knives to Sharpen!

I got sea crabs! I got sea crabs!

Fresh Fish Today!

I've go-ot ice he-er!

2¢ Ices!

Swe-eet Potatoes!

Cockles and Mussels!

Rags For Sale!

Tooma luma luma
Tooma luma luma
Toodle aye aa!

"*I WANNA BE A PART OF IT...*"

On the #1 train, an older man plays his horn
and a recorded music box, while holding a cup
for contributions. Down the aisle, from the other
end, comes a young man with no legs, propelling
his chair. "How ya doin', Alex?" asks the older
man with a horn. "Hey, it's New York," answers
the young man with no legs. The older man nods
and plays "If I can make it here, I'll make it
anywhere."

EXIT, PURSUED BY BEAR

When I was paid
to wear a mask,

I lauded authenticity,
off-stage, as well as on,

transparency, the open
book, the open vein: my song.

All the world is still
a stage, though I'm a different player.

It seems the mask works just as well
off-stage as it works on,

taming that unruly shrew
we nick-name honesty.

LYING ABOUT SEX

"Elizabeth, I have confessed"
John Proctor,
The Crucible, Arthur Miller

I thought I saw
my husband

What of Abigail Williams?

somewhat turning from

Goody Proctor

My husband is a good
and righteous

To your own knowledge,
has John Proctor

I came to think
he fancied

Your husband —
did he

My husband
is a goodly

Then he
did not

He is a goodly

Has John Proctor ever
committed the crime

He

Is your husband
a lecher?

No, Sir.

Captive Audience

"Talk To Me Like The Rain
And Let Me Listen"
—Tennessee Williams

1.
In the play, it's The Man
who asks her
to talk to him. Yes
is all The Woman says.
No one worries
about role reversal:
It's a play.

2.
The Woman does not say
Talk to Me.
You never talk to me.
The Man says he will lie
there and listen
if The Woman will
just talk to him.

3.
I will always lie
there and listen
when The Man uses words
righter even than rain.
If he lies,
I will love
each perfect word.

PUT THE BLAME ON MAINE

1.
After Bette left him,
(After *All About Eve*),
Gary stayed in our home
town, drinking more and more,
strolling the length of the piers,
rarely stopping to buy a lobster.

2.
Before she left him, Bette Davis
directed our Christmas Pageant,
commanding miniature lords and ladies
to sword and garland dance
with zest, to carry
a paper-mâché boar's head, while singing
"The Boar's Head Carol," then exiting
with "Joy to the World."

3.
When Gary's heart began
to heal, he drank
a little less, was seen
around town a little more,
each event a rehearsal for that
starry starry day
Gary Merrill took Rita Hayworth
to the Bowdoin-Williams game.

PAUL AND JOANNE

"Last of the great broads,"
he called her, and when he left
the world, he'd been with the broad
for fifty years, from The Long Hot Summer,
From the Terrace, Rachel, Rachel,
Mr. and Mrs. Bridge: Winning.
It may not all have been a Picnic,
but theirs was a story to love.

Necessary for love is memory.
Seven years later,
she's now lost most
of both, but still remembers this:
"I used to be married to someone very handsome."

"AND THAT HAS MADE ALL THE DIFFERENCE"

When Robert Mitchum and Jimmy Stewart
died within one day of each other
it became clear
that every choice or accident
had brought me to this
moment of unavoidable recognition
that the world was divided
between Robert Mitchum people
and Jimmy Stewart people
and I was Robert Mitchum people
and I'd been having one hell
of a wonderful life.

COSTUMES

My mother made mine
until I played a whore,
that summer in *Three Penny Opera*.
It was the short black skirt
she had to slit
all the way up my thigh, not
the fish-net stockings,
or the fuck-me pumps
that stopped her. She didn't have to
make them. I could buy
the stockings in my father's store, or
rather, he could buy them, and I could borrow
her pumps, which I still have.
She's dead five years now, but when
the doctors were keeping her alive,
they had to amputate her still
comely leg, above the knee. When
we had to empty her home,
we found even more shoes
than I remembered, although
she'd stopped shopping for anything
else years before and never
went anywhere. "You can tell a well-dressed woman
by her shoe wardrobe," she
used to tell me.
My father told me
he first saw her in a play
called *Street Scene*, or
was it *Cry Havoc*?
She played in both.

FOUND: WILDE CINQUAIN

"To lose
one parent may
be regarded as a
misfortune. To lose both looks like
carelessness."

STAGE DIRECTIONS FOR FATHER'S DAY

Paint toes red.
Think only twelve times of the hospital bed.
Polish the wit
When the images hit.

WHO DO YOU THINK YOU ARE,

Sarah Bernhardt? Jewish
parents, apparently in addition
to mine, loved to pop as a question,
which, being Jewish, was really
an answer disguised as a question:
"You with the drama,
enough already!" My mother
acted, on stage and off;
my father acted like he wished
he were in the audience. I became
an actor, and missed his last
hours upon the stage
that all the world is,
because I had a second audition
for a show,
which must go on.

NOTES

'A green and yellow melancholy' - 'Smiling at grief. Was not this love indeed?'—*Twelfth Night*, William Shakespeare

Sweet Songs of the Street—Written in collaboration with Poets and Writers Workshop, Stanley Isaacs Center, N.Y.

Exit, pursued by bear—stage direction in *The Winter's Tale*, William Shakespeare

ACKNOWLEDGMENTS

Thanks to the editors of the publications/books in which these poems originally appeared:

A Little Beckett, A Little O'Neill	*Big City Lit*
	Transfiguration Begins at Home, Tiger Bark Press
As I look down on you, I love you	*Maine Arts Journal*
Performance Art	*at the last minute*, Salmon Poetry
Exit, pursued by bear	*at the last minute*, Salmon Poetry
Lying About Sex	*JJournal*
	at the last minute, Salmon Poetry
Captive Audience	*at the last minute*, Salmon Poetry
Paul and Joanne	*at the last minute*, Salmon Poetry;
	Like Light 25 Years of Poetry and Prose, Bright Hill Press
'And that has made all the difference'	*Transfiguration Begins at Home*, Tiger Bark Press
Found: Wilde Cinquain (first stanza of poem called *Found: Wilde Cinquains*)	*at the last minute*, Salmon Poetry
Costumes	*Transfiguration Begins at Home*, Tiger Bark Press
Stage Directions for Father's Day	*at the last minute*, Salmon Poetry
Who do you think you are,	*at the last minute*, Salmon Poetry
	Like Light 25 Years of Poetry and Prose, Bright Hill Press

About the Author

ESTHA WEINER is the author of *at the last minute* (Salmon Poetry), *In the Weather of the World* (Salmon Poetry), *The Mistress Manuscript* (Asheville Book Works), *Transfiguration Begins At Home* (Tiger Bark Press); and co-editor/contributor to *Blues for Bill: A Tribute to William Matthews* (Akron Poetry Series, University of Akron Press). Her poems have appeared in numerous anthologies and magazines, including *The New Republic* and *Barrow Street*. Winner of a Paterson Poetry Prize and a Visiting Scholar at The Shakespeare Institute, Stratford, England, she is founding director of Sarah Lawrence College NY Alumni/ae Writers Nights, Marymount Writers Nights, and a Speaker on Shakespeare for The New York Council For The Humanities. She is a Professor in the English Department at City College of New York and Sarah Lawrence College Writing Institute, and serves or has served on the Poetry/Writing faculties of The Frost Place, Hudson Valley Writers Center, Stone Coast Writers Conference, Poets and Writers, Poets House, and The Writers Voice. She also serves on the Advisory Committee of Slapering Hol Press, Hudson Valley Writers Center. In her previous life, she was an actor and worked for BBC Radio.